# Reign Drops

SUMMER BURNETT

PUBLISHED BY FIDELI PUBLISHING, INC.

Copyright © 2017 by Summer Burnett

All rights reserved.
No part of this publication may be reproduced, stored in a retrieval system or transmitted in any way by any means, electronic, mechanical, photocopy, recording or otherwise, without the prior permission of the author, except as provided by USA copyright law.

ISBN: 978-1-60414-970-8

Cover photo by Barry Cook

# Dedication

For everyone I've ever loved.
If I ever loved you, I will always love you.

# Authors Bio

New erotic fiction author Summer Alana Reign is just what the doctor ordered to ignite and heat up your sensuality! Summer began exploring the world of erotica as a talk show host of the internet radio show, The Reign Drop, where she interviewed many authors including New York Times Best-Selling author Zane.

Summer brings a fresh spin to poetry by saturating the minds of the reader with lyrical illusions as they are taken on a sensual roller coaster that will leave the reader asking for more.

When "The Queen of Wetness" is not enticing good girls and guys out of their comfort zones with her poetry, she can be found traveling and spending quality time with her daughter, family and friends.

Born in Newark, Ohio, Summer Reign is the oldest of her mothers' four daughters.

She graduated with a B.A. in Communications and Theatre from Ohio Dominican University in 1999.

Summer lives her life to the fullest with no regrets.

# Acknowledgments

It's been a long time coming and so many of you have stuck in my corner waiting on the release of this book for many years, and for that, I THANK YOU. To GOD be the glory, and I THANK HIM!!!

To everyone who has ever took the time to listen when I called excited to share my words over the phone no matter the time, I THANK YOU.

To Method Man, REDMAN and the whole crew, I kept my ears open when you were teaching me the ropes, even when you didn't realize you were doing so. I appreciate the love that you have shown to both me and my daughter and I will never forget it. Thank you for being such awesome big brothers, role models and inspirations along my journey with you all, I THANK YOU.

Sadat X, me being able to listen to your old school stories and watching you chase your entrepreneur dreams has done more for me than you will ever know, I THANK YOU.

B-Real (my SWAM), Terri Whitlow, Greatness, Wawa, Croomy, Robbie, Ms. Walker, MegaPhone and Tia Stewart (no one asked for this book more than you, girrrrrrrl), you all have been my glue throughout this process and I wouldn't be in this place if any ONE of you were missing. I love you all and I THANK YOU.

To every Droplet and to ALL the Original Droplets, I THANK YOU.

To everyone that has ever served as a muse for me, both knowing and unknowingly :) I THANK YOU.

To all my family and friends who have been an influence in any way, or who have supported, or who will support, my heart opens up and thanks you all, in a huge way.

To everyone who has ever had the desire to love, show love, be love or exude love proudly…I THANK YOU!

# Table of Contents

*Authors Bio* ................................................................................ *v*
*Acknowledgments* .................................................................. *vii*

Gentle Kisses ............................................................................ 1
Weekend Getaway .................................................................... 2
Sweet Daydream ....................................................................... 3
Do Me ........................................................................................ 5
Summer Reign ........................................................................... 8
Foxy .......................................................................................... 10
Curiosity ................................................................................... 12
Me and My Guy ....................................................................... 14
Say My Name .......................................................................... 16
Wicked Grinds ......................................................................... 17
 Energy ..................................................................................... 18
Do You Know? ........................................................................ 20
He Is Different ......................................................................... 23
My Promise .............................................................................. 24
Please, Sit Down ..................................................................... 26
Shhhh... ................................................................................... 28
Polaroids .................................................................................. 30
Quickie ..................................................................................... 32
Subtle Kisses ........................................................................... 33
Wishes ..................................................................................... 35
New Beginnings ...................................................................... 36
Sho Nuff .................................................................................. 37

Last Night .......................................................................................... 38
Lose Control .................................................................................... 40
Tasty Treats .................................................................................... 42
Wait .................................................................................................. 44
Simplicity ........................................................................................ 45
Throat Hugging .............................................................................. 47
Head Games .................................................................................... 48
Can't Swim ...................................................................................... 49
I Still Taste You .............................................................................. 50
Let You Go ...................................................................................... 53
Alignement ...................................................................................... 55
Big Fan ............................................................................................. 56
Only Gets Better ............................................................................. 58
Tension ............................................................................................. 60

# Gentle Kisses

The subtle mist of WET poetry, entices me…
So Delighting to me….
It sparks this crazy feeling inside of me….
Gentle KISSES on notebooks filled with lines…

I'll hypnotize your mind with my pen's 3rd eye…
With soft caresses your mental undresses…
In preparation to be turned out…

U see…I can indeed fulfill every VERBAL fantasy…
& occasionally bring your thoughts to orgasm…

I'm just asking that you keep up…
Showing you is not enough…

Because I know you need to hear it….
so I'll make love to your spirit….
And Foreplay with these LYRICS!!!!!

# Weekend Getaway

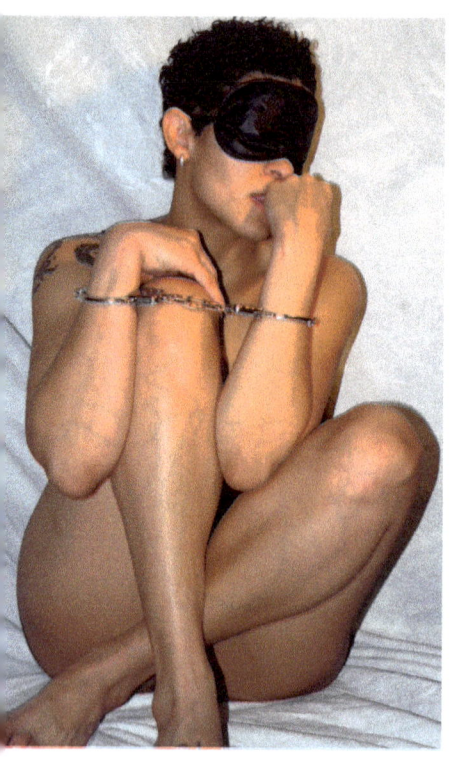

What would a weekend get you?
With me in the bed with you?

Laid up…. bodies shifting
Glazed up start to finish…
Pleasing you is my main interest…
Pleading to act out the vision…
Wrestle not, with your decisions…
Neva stop my grinding missions…

My kitty's cumin with precision…
I'll play with her…and then I'll lick it…
Cum in my mouth
like my life's depending…

Your favorite porn scene re-lived
and everything you wanted to
but never did…

Begging for things…
like whips and shit…
Passion turns into viciousness…
and Intentions become relentless when…
We're face to face and missioning…

Place you in a state of make believe.
Almost like…you're pretending it…
Don't wanna believe its real living…
Both of us taking…
and both of us giving….

# Sweet Daydream

Sweet daydreamin'
about off the wall occasions
Strictly fantasies
A lot of role playin'.

Guessing what you like to hear...
And how you want me to say it...

I bet you want me to touch u
there...even...

Play with it...and taste it...
Be a bitch you can't compare...
I don't do shit basic...

Neva, have you once...
Wrote ya name with cum...
On a bitch face while she tastes it...

Make a movie just for fun...

Turn around and then replay it...
Keep my kitty extra clean...
every otha day I'm shavin'....

Get you to just that point...
Make you feel like you can't take it...
Then...straddle you up on the chair...
So we...can face to face it...

I know you really wanna hit...
But let me just test your patience.
And I know you really wanna get...

A little closer to relations...

But how about I just stand up...
Turn around and then spank it...
Bend down and...

Touch my toes for you...
Say something while I shake it...
Twerk it like I'm supposed to do...


In case u were mistaken...
Ain't another bitch like me...
The rest of them are fakin'...

But this is just a daydream...
About off the wall occasions.

# Do Me

Do me...baby tonight...
And get my mind excited...
For what has never happened...

Or maybe it has. But not this good...
Never once this good....
These feelings...
So...anticipated...
So...expected...

I've estimated the amount of time...
That it will take for you...
To get me to that point...
Where.... where...my love overflows...
All over you...
Do me...baby tonight...
Like, there's a check at the end...
Waiting for you...
With overtime and bonuses...
And shit...included...

Do me baby...tonight...
Like. Like you were sent from above...
To explore every erotic zone that I possess....
And was mandated...by God... Herself...
To report blow by blow...
So that she too...could get hers...

Do me...baby...Tonight...
Like. Like...mission impossible...
'Cuz this mission's so plausible....
So, probable...
That there's nothing in the way that could even stop you...

Attack me so persistently...
That I scream for you to stop and go...
At the same time....
I mean... Harass me in every way u fantasized about...

Do me. Baby...Tonight...
Like...your lips were sliced right in the middle....
For this sole...purpose...
Or ...for my soul's purpose...

Do me... Like...tonight is your last night
On this Beautiful place, we call...
King Sized Bed...

Like...like...sometimes you forget that
You and I are not actually physically attached...
And that...it doesn't even matter to you...
Do me...baby...tonight...
Like the party ain't over
And it never will be...

Do me. Baby. Tonight.
Like...Teddy Riley told you to...
And that you owed him your life...

Like when you stop...
Like...when you take that last lick...
Your tongue won't even work again...

Do me... like...I did something to you...
And take it personal...
Like my shit just talked about ya Mama...

Do me…like…like…
U got weapons of mass destruction…
And you know where they are...
And you know how to use them...

Do me like…I've got every answer
To your every problem…
And you just gotta dig to find 'em…

Do me…baby…like….
I never asked you to do anything before…
And that…
you were just waiting for me to open my mouth…
To say something…

Do me. Like. Like…You always do…
But just Do ME…Tonight … BABY!!!

## Summer Reign

My mouth waters to the sweet taste
of your fantasies...
Bump'n Nasty mental imageries...
simplicity induced...
Followed by moments of truth...
Time will stand...
Completely still, since I took it...

In search of,
Your fountain of youth...
Your happiness I pursue
& Insist on mind kissing,
U're intellect,

Insinuating passion persistently...
The fact of the matter...

U can't control
how you're into me...
I deliberately display
Moments of sensitivity,
irrational probabilities...

And OMG, my mind is on U...
But like to the 10th degree...
As long as I live...
so will u're memory...

And I promise to give a little more
than everything
and Will never pretend
you're less than the world...
influencing my body movements...

Toes curled...Back arched...
If foreplay is an art...
Then I'm Moaning LISA...
and Thou art...my Donatello...

My whole being desires to be...
Wherever you go...

I exhale with focus...
& Put my words in slow motion...
So, rare & new...I
'm surprised...
Close my eyes & see your image behind my lids...

Blind to any existing imperfections...
You're an ideal candidate of my mirrored reflection...
My heart's covered by the protection of your Warmth and compassion...

Ultimate satisfaction...
In awe by your actions...
The swagger inside you is so relaxin'...
The words you use...have me climaxin'...
Changing my drawls...
I applaud...
Your mysterious demeanor has me climbin' up walls.
Your composition has me so involved.

So into your energy...with positive force...
and of course I'm into you too with no remorse...
Lighting the fire to my torch...so...

I can stay on my course...
I thank you so much...
It's with love...I endorse....
Summer Reign

# Foxy

A total foxy situation...
Got my whole body vibratin'...
See me in my French maid...
Doin' some role playin'...

See me bend real low,
so you can spank it while I

Shake it...

"Do it daddy" With a soft chuckle while I say it...
Strip real slow...

To where I'm almost naked...
Let ya mind wander...
So you can get creative...

Put me in some shit.
Where I almost can't escape
& Turn, the camera on
So when we're done we can replay it...

Light the candles...
So you can...See right where I'm layin'...

If you can handle the shit...
I'm about to bring, then you already know it's raining...
I'm saying... quit playin'...

I'm gamin...doin' much more than maintaining.

So...tonight...let's just, throw away shame...
and bring pain...for fun...

A small concussion…
From aggressive lusting...
Spontaneous combustions,
when our bodies are thrusting…

I hear harmonies of
Lovely melodic percussions…
my blood starts rushin'…
my kitty's gushin'…until the day's end...

But you and I know...
it all started with a total foxy situation!!!!!!!!!!!

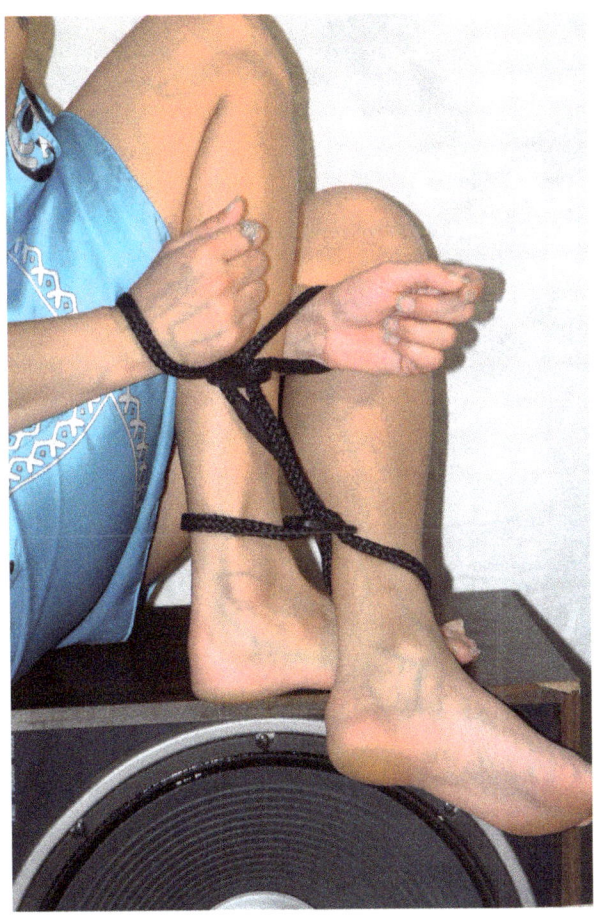

# Curiosity

When I walk into a room ure curiosity's uplifted…
I'm gifted at shift'n and ure imagination is listenin'…
Creatin' fantasies of us in my kitchen…

Of you makin' love like ya mad at me. Like I am ya bitch and…

Pull my hair emphatically
until my thighs start to glisten…
She already down there twitchin'…&

U lol'n but I'm not even kiddin'…

When I imagine, us kissing…
my head begins spinning…
U make love to my vision…
while leading the way to my mission…
My unfallen king…with his Crown in position…
Dominating my flesh…
holding my limbs in suspension…

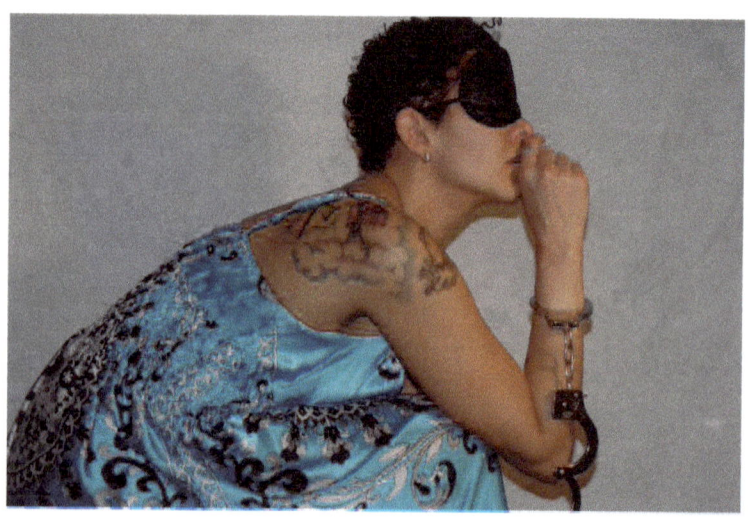

Ohhh...but the ultimate twist is…
I love the way we FUCK...
I be creatin' positions...
throw it back every time….
no matter how I'm bent & swallow ya whole…
and burp up...Ya children…

It's on when I'm wet...
like a fucking gremlin…
cum on ya Dick…
Like hurricane relentless…
Flood up the gates until we fuckin swimmin'…

U think it's over,
but it's just the beginning…

# Me and My Guy

His smile is pleasant.
Receiving it…is like taking hold of a million blessings…
The ultimate test is…
Not turning away…but being his reflection…
Following his direction.

I'm a slave to his erection…
Swallow his kids with perfection…
Look, no hands before intimate wrestling…
then lick his ear with soft sweet confessions…
Grind on his leg until he gets my message…

Holding…the headboard for ultimate leverage…
Bout to soak u daddy with your favorite beverage…
Shit…he said…as long as he had a face…
I gotta…Place to sit
And I'm done holding back…so I'm about to lose it…
and soak the room…

Quick…
Tie me up with blindfolds and feed me juices…
Mangoes mixed in with what he produces…
and Tangos to sensual music…

Our bodies connected… in a lust filled fusion…
Eyes rolled back…like there's some confusion…
but we're fully aware of optical illusions…

Like… every time I bust…the fucking room spins…
with every single thrust…My soul shakes when he moves in…
and out…
with precision…hitting spots…so deliberate….

Convincing myself…this is something…I could live with…
Damn…daddy giving me the business…

He set up shop…
and now he BOUT to vend it…
And Flip it...& Flip me…

Cuz see…we...fly high...
Create our love in the sky…
I lay on the clouds….
Me and my Guy.

# Say My Name

How do I love thee? Let me count the ways…

The way you…Say my name…say my name…when you bust….
The way…Ya dick trembles…in the deep of my guts…
The way…Your eyes roll back while I suck on ya nuts.

The way…Mother nature don't change…so then you adjust…
The way…You coat my nails…because you care enough… &
The way…You pick me up to make love…like it's nuthin'…
The way…You rub my feet I go crazy…no frontin'…
The way…I daydream about you…and blush &..

The way…you get my picture mails…and start touchin'…even
The way Ya name appears on my phone…excites something…. Damn…

The way… your voice is foreplay…
The way… I can't want you…in no worst way…

The way…our bodies fall perfectly…when we do lay…and embrace…
The way I fall asleep first…with a smile on my face…
The way these words hit the paper…with ease…from my brain…
The way…even if I could…none of our history would be erased…

From the bad to the good…humility pays…
The way we Operate best in a smaller space…
The way…We motivate each other to win the race…and
The way we Have the utmost respect for each other's pace. I love you… And

I still haven't even started counting the ways….

# Wicked Grinds

Lyrically wicked grinds...
Exchanging lines...in poetic fashion...
Making love to my mind...

Straight ninja assassin...
proper noun...
and verb action...
Stimulating nerves...
Mentally Climaxing...
Long discussions leave...
my head in ya lap...
A new-found habitat...
I'm home...
Where my daddy at?

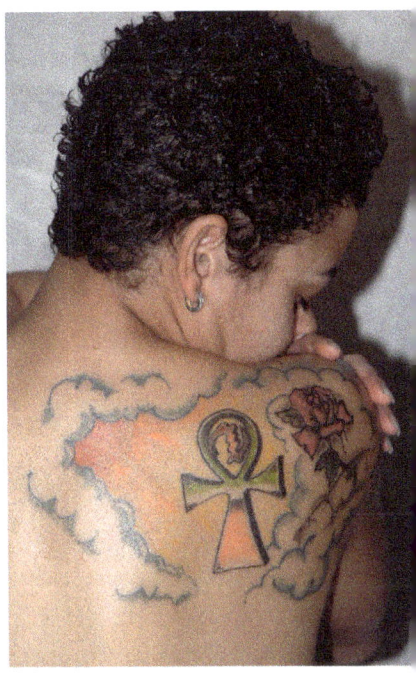

Allow me to caress you with foot rubs...
And happy chats...
Crack the window...And let the rain drop on the small of my back...
Exposing my tats...
We throw our heads back and laugh...

Your pointy finger on my stomach
turns into autographs...invisibly planting flags...
U complete me...without having to ask...

Nose dives into warm milk and honey baths...
Super powers without the mask...

You carry me away...Cal-gone...my ass...
We make love thru the splish-splashes...

I drop low...
And then flip it fast....

# Energy

See, you can't even handle my kisses…
Look atcha self…makin such stupid decisions…
I admit it…they vicious…
You admit they're delicious…
One thing we can agree on… Is u'd be down…
if I was with it…

I sleep sound when I'm finished…
After I give you the business…
3 or 4 times in my mouth…gotchu…
Bustin' ridiculous…and just know…

I shift when I'm giving…
and when I'm Riding I'm spinning…
Throw you in the back of my throat
so Relentless…

Have you stand back and look in my face…
Like "you trippin'"
We both would start gigglin'…

I'd show you that I'm dripping…
Then lick my fingers…to get back to my clitoris…

Bend over backwards...
Twist...shift my position...
Scream outloud....my outrageous opinions...

Gotcha clutchin' my waist
So that you grind with precision...
Damn... "Give it to me, daddy!"
Can't help but moan while you hit it....

Lost in a zone...so fuckin suspended...
& I don't wanna stop...
so baby...please...
Don't finish...

I'm trainin' you to CUM...with my permission...
No hands...and all tongue...sexy visions...
Ball up when I'm done...
In a fetal position, G...
Cuz I swallowed ya sons and ya daughters So willingly.

Light bulbs pop up...
Cuz my ideas hit brilliantly...
And never leave you unfulfilled
Cuz ya girl's got that ENERGY.

# Do You Know?

When I think about how bad I want You...
My mouth waters...
My...kitty pulsates...
My...complete...body aches for your touch...

I'm genuinely in love.
With how you make me feel...
I don't' get it twisted...or confused with the real...

Cuz see...I already know that I can't have you...
Not for myself...you're the type of Brotha...
That every woman should sample at least once...
In her lifetime...

A moment of pure passion...
Bodies thrashing...Multiple orgasms...
If only for this one night...
Please...don't be polite
with how you treat me...

See...I want you to get down on one knee...
I do...
Not want you to pop the question...
But pop my body...
Teach me some lessons...

Make it hard for me to breathe...
Make it hard to believe...
That this is one man. On top of me....
Caressing...
Suggesting...Different positions...

See…when I think about how bad I want you…
I imagine inventing new ways to turn myself…
Out of proportion shit….
Professional contortionist…

I imagine engaging you for a night...
One night filled with...
The rawest delight…you've ever received…
I aim to please...

Unlimited measures...
Giver of pleasure…
Wanna talk dirty…
Fuck it...shit...Hurt me…
Harder…

Would that make your manhood grow larger?
Don't bother playing shy...
Nah... baby…tonight's...not that night….

We're grown up in here….
Give me something I can hear…
Scream some nasty shit in my Ears...
Like...Bitch…Your pussy...
Is so…relentless...
I'mma kill this shit...4 times...

Before we end this….
Please, Grab my hair…
And stop pretending...

Every once in a while…
Go slow…
But mostly act…
Like it's a race you winning…

Fuck me like…
You did in your mind…before this moment…
When you jacked off in the shower…
So that first one wouldn't blow it…

And when you're done…
After you busted…
I wanna taste on you…
Cuz I don't trust it…

I know you got another one…Somewhere in you….
Somewhere there are a million more little sperms…
Waiting to be released…

And we can go all night…
To ensure they get free...
Cuz…one way or another...
They are welcome in me…

I don't discriminate…
Slide 'em down my throat…
Baby…please…believe…I don't play….

So, when I think about…
How bad I want to...
How bad I long too...
Touch and suck…
And fuck...and CUM too...
You're right on my mind…every time…
And that's cool!!!

# He Is Different

How does he hold me so different…?
To where: his arms feel like magic…
I've questioned to his face… His voodoo tactics…

When I back into him something Fantastic…his eyebrows raise up…
And he looks down at what's happening…
And I wouldn't dare pretend…that he is anyone else but him…
Why? Well…
Because he holds me so different.

Some chicks…wish they could feel this…
His leg fits perfect in between my thighs…and his lips…
Lay on the back of my neck with soft breaths…
Down my spine…

When we lay…he wraps his…
Everything around me…and we sleep soundly…
Night after night…he holds me so different…

My whole-body quivers…every time…we touch…
I used to push him away…Cuz a little seemed like too much…
Now…no matter what I do…
I can't get enough…

I guess it's true what they say…
You know when it's…. *breath*
Cuz he holds me so different…plus… He is my favorite…

And My sound clips…display it…he's found new ways… To be patient…
And I make sweet love to his mind…while his body waits…
And when we do Cum together… it feels like…
We busting in space…jump off of him…and Kiss the fuck out his face…
I'm feeling this cat…what more could I say?

# My Promise

Would you like to Fuck?
Or, excuse me...Make love?
Right here where we are...or in the back of some club?

My body starts to shake instant....
Reminiscing our past moments...and how we pretended...
Role playing scenarios...actin out our own wish lists...

Shit...that last time you dicked me down so good...
Until we finished...cummin' at the same time...yeah
That's the business...becuz every moan you made...my kitty kat listened...
She responds Soakin' wet...I mean...that mutha fucka...be glistenin'...
Catchin' you off guard...becuz my juices flow endless...

Let's jump in the back of the whip...on some kid shit...or face each other hips taste test...69ish...would you like that? Or how about this?

Break into my house...with handcuffs and whips...
Create a situation where naughty exists...
like YOU bout to just man up and... take it...shut me up... And degrade it...
then leave out the window... With me layin there naked...

And if that ain't ya thing...Officer Reign on the way then...
I'll read you your rights…then slap on...your bracelets...
Let you break free...just for the chase...

It's your world…you see…if you dream...
I'm on stage...or re-enact...the old days...
You be Ike…and I'll be Tina...sexy ass...foreplay…
I know it sounds crazy…but even she stayed...for the Longest…
Don't judge if you ain't on it...
Create a new situation...a French maid...Or a farmer…
I'll be ya dirty little sum...for a Few extra dollas…
let you choke hold my throat...
To quiet my holla…

Or leave ransom notes
Some hide & seek in the closet…

See…it's whateva you wish…
I'm so down. That's my promise…

# Please, Sit Down

Sit the fuck down & relax me please…
I'm talking about right now…
Climax your main squeeze…

Let me exhale my release…
Put some buckle in my knees…
Twist my hair around your fingers and proceed lightly…

Sit the fuck down…before…we start fighting….
Please? That's twice I've asked nicely…
Politely.

Now…I apologize in advance if my
Ways aren't inviting or exciting…
The reality of the situation is…I need to bust nightly…

And now that you're home DADDY ….
Sit the fuck down…
And put your babies inside me…

Inside of my mouth….right there on the couch…
Assume ya favorite position and let me.
Caress ya arouse… Suggest that somehow…I taste…
While upside down…
And swallow not waste…all of the first round…
Make you proud of ya desires…
Then press my chest against ya crown…

Damn…sit the fuck down…
Please…maybe switch it up…
Let YOUR tongue roam…on me…humph….
Let you…can't lick enough…
Let me…can't bust too much…

Run it down…ya chin… & the crack of my stuff…
Bodies…soaking…wet…waterfalls…of love-juices…
Race to the wet spot…like the fountain of youth…

Shiiiit! Intoxicating fluids…like I'm drunk…
While we do it…
Must be the funk…

Cuz you're my bass in love music.
Now, how's that sound?

Whatever you do...just please…please…
Sit…the fuck…DOWN!!!!

# Shhhh…

Ohhh…you can't tell me nuthin…
Not with your mouth…
No, tonight…Let your actions say something….
Let your hands scream…
Real loud…Know what I'm talkin' about?

Let ya fingers whisper sweet nothings…
ALL OVER MY BODY...
Shhhh….quiet like a charades party…

Heavy breathing…with thoughts…so naughty…
1st word...2 syllables…
I'm acting out crazy…'cuz this feelings so sensual…
And I know I'm a sexual individual but…
Go slow…As the spirit jumps into you….
And let it seduce ya mental and physical…
Or else what's the use for mixing our chemicals…?

As I swallow ya youth, my kitty cat trembles...
cuz she's long overdue for you to run up in her…

After, you release the swimmers....
Down the back of my throat...
Yeah...i'mma winner... I swallow fa sho...'til I make you surrender...

You used to BEG for more...from ole girl...Remember?
But I be on it... on you...and
Ohhh...the way you respond....to my touch... FUCK!...

Instant jump up...
Causing my blood to pump sum...serious...
Fa real...
And tonight...this is the deal...
No words...let our tongues...feel
for new erotic zones...
On their own free will...

Deal? Are you down?
Let's create new boundaries
Or explore their endless limits....

My head's spinning...
In awe of this sexual friendship...

# Polaroids

Let's say we create or retell a story with pictures...
No words...but ya eyes still listen...
As Polaroid freeze frames...Replace naughty descriptions...

On the cover would be me as a princess...
Butt-naked with rose pedals...demanding attention...
And as you open...no table of contents... (Let's be honest)
You wouldn't even want to ruin the fun...

Remember slow tease with visual penetrations?
Mastering the sensation...&

You really do wanna hold on to this moment
but ya finger can't wait...
And begins to turn page...

& There I go...there I go...there I go...again...
A head shot of my face...but something is Missing...
Looking into my eyes...

Something sho is different...
Confusion appears and my face is twisted...
And as you try and imagine...what's on my mind...

The next page is flippn'. The next Polaroid depicts...
A full body shot... Me in position...karma sutra image...

Against the wall...and you close your eyes and wish....
And as you turn the page...
The still shot includes...me holding a whip...
and Whip cream...drips across my lips...handcuffs lay exposed..
And shit....

Your hands start roaming across ya dick…
Anticipating…the next luxurious pic…
And now…I have my toy with my tongue against it…
Creatin' new found joys to rise inside your existence….

Behold…a beautiful woman…struggling with being tempted…
As you laugh…and grab a hold of ya shit…and pretend…It's you…
Then lick ya finger, anxious to see… The image…
On the otha side of the sheet… Blinkin' so hard you can't fuckin believe.

"My toy" up inside, my legs bent so weak.
And my juices captured…flowing in one long…Squirted stream….
So you bring the book closer…cock ya head regain focus…

Damn you REIGN…everything is explosive….
Better than slow…still shots…no motion….
The final pic of the watch and a road…
It lets you know now daddy that it's time to cum home...

Let's you know
Now...
It's time...
To
Cum...
Home!!!

# Quickie

Right now...I strongly desire a quickie...
for someone to quickly enter and shift me....
Some manhood inside my walls...instantly re-inventing...
Just for the hell of it...just because.....

The next man I see...or the next one that calls...
I'mma put it on him...
I'mma give him my all...

Now don't judge me by far...
Cuz I want to get off...
Just point me in the right direction to start...

If you know me at all you know,
I embrace all of my flaws...

Oral fixate these jaws...
The sensation remains 4
Something right now 2 jump off...

Make it more than a thought, actually put him on every part
Of my essence....for however long we hold on...
Like 4 minutes...and 20 sum seconds...

Of makin love reckless...

# Subtle Kisses

Subtle kisses...sweet, straight...from ya misses...
Relax divine sensations....ya foreplay's amazing...
The way ya hands caress my thighs and legs...
And dead give a-ways...when my limbs...start to shake...

You rattle and roll me...out of control we...
Move towards ecstasy, allowing our minds...
To be free...as our bodies release...at the same time...
Orgasms seep...and soak the sheets...and I Lean and whisper...
"Tell me what you're thinking?"

This Summer Reign has ya tweaking...bobble head weak...
2 sweaty freaks, lite ice please...

Ya smile...entices me...to pull you tightly...
Sing...lullaby's...swing low...sweet chariot...
See...close ya eyes and...give in to my likings...
Let's make love like we're fighting...
Pull my hair with soft biting...
and no Disrespect...when I cuss you out right?
Unbelievably right...

At night its sweet dreams at the same time...
And in the morning...steak and eggs...over white wine...

Lust or love is a fine line…let's walk it out… And recite rhymes.
Remember back in the old times?

Dry humping…and slow grinds?
Daaaamn… You take me to a place…where…we…are Secluded…
in my own mind…

It's just me…and you while the sun rises…
And rays of light… Brighten the night…

As the next day…arrives…&
Subtle kisses…relay the right time…
To get started again…
First with plug and play toys…and then some giga-biting.

# Wishes

What if every wish could come true?
If everything you ever thought you could do?
Things would never be the same….That's the truth!

Have control over my emotions…and my actions…too.
Wish me to subject you to verbal abuse…
Then wish for some brains to wash my mouth with some you…
Make me a bad lil mommy…All the things you would do.

Ohhh, would you wish for unlimited sex…?
Sun up to sun down…hot, sticky, wet…
*Breath*
Then sun down to sun up…ruff, kinky, bet?

Wish me to travel the world with you… Meditate in Tibet?
Wish your all I adore is you…Wish for daily taste tests..?
Would you wish I'd massage you from the back with my breasts?
Peek-a-boo ya eyes…then soft scrape ya chest….

If everyone of your wishes came true…
Would your 1st one…unite…me to you?
Would your next one tie up my limbs?  Speak the truth?

What's the use of holding them in..?
I mean…if they could cum to life… If you could MAKE me GIVE in…

Shit…
I wish you could be so privileged
and take me out of my zone with boundaries so
ENDLESS…

But if you don't…I STILL have a freaky lil wish list.

# New Beginnings

Have you ever wanted his STUFF so bad?
You damn near...cum on yourself ...at the sight...
Of his mustache? LOL...shit...

Sex addict status...and be tweaking....
When some bass hits my eardrums...
While at it...everything sounds nasty...when I wanna cum...

Playing with myself...over long conversations...
Between me...and I Get off...
Damn near shameful like...maybe that's why...no one...
Wants to talk about mastering...it...

Calling out my own name...pretending...that's him slapping it...
I mean...me... across my cheeks...leaving prints...

Excuse me...while my imagination vents...
Because I've wanted him so bad for so long...

And like Janet spit...I don't even know if he knows that I exist...
Does he even know if I'm alive?
Cuz my kitty lets me know...every time he walks by...
She get to jumping with delight...both sets of lips...
Start trying to check mics...

What? Shit...All I'm just saying...
Ahh...forget it. It's just...I do more than daydream about him...
I actually go home... and act out my Visions...
Bring them shits...to life. Minus him...

But me and I love pretending... Role play to the ending...
Usually with a shower scene...but that just creates new beginnings...

# Sho Nuff

I whisper ya name in the tub when I cum…
And pull the shower head down…2…just for fun…
Let it go like a mic…superstar when I'm done…
Record my moans…play them back on every station…

Without my kitty in your mouth…too much time is being wasted…
I'm really excited…and you are testing my patience…

I'm 'bout to put my hands on you…something flagrant…
Leo to the core…to forgets a mistake…

I wanna Jump on it…and ride you, let you make…my milkshake…
Let, "Who's going to cum first?" be our biggest debate…

Ego's at stake….and hearts are racing…
Put a mirror on the ceiling so our images are facing…
Back at us… Sexy status…

In ya mouth like a breathing apparatus…
On the couch…like some fucking jack rabbits.
We winning bouts…got belts…

And mango platters…in my mind you like to tie me up…
And feed me… While you're jabbing…

Put ya fingers in my mouth…and drive me crazy…
While we are at it…and I'll whisper you soft poetry in ya ear…
Sit back and let me Freestyle my habits…

Make sure that you hear everything that matters…
Cuz I'm not going to stop until you're screaming…
I'm…the….baddest!!!!!!!!!!!!

# Last Night

Last night was so…Intoxicating.
Insane sensations penetrated every essence of my being…
From my toes in your mouth, to leaning over the couch…

Back flashes still causing shivers to arouse.
We experimented with all 5 senses somehow…
Chocolate, incense, blindfolds,
& Reign in the background…

From the kitchen to the bathroom.
The balcony and then back down.
I know I screamed your name so loud…
I know I came hard in, ya mouth…
Cuz I bout…damn near…passed out…

And even now…when I think about…
How my legs were curled around…
And how our bodies created sound.
Damn it…

If only I would have recorded that shit…
I'd Cut the audio and paste some lyrics, over our moans
but under the spirit. Harmonious tones to a utopian feeling,
and my mind is gone…

I'm so lost in him… I Held my thoughts within…but my juices…
Wouldn't even pretend…had his leg soaking…
Words wouldn't come out…caught up in my throat and…
I knew that it wouldn't last forever but I sure was hoping…
That this memory won't die…moments of now…
Turn into thoughts for a lifetime…

And this seems like the right time... To grind again with you all night...
My mind veers off...and begins to take flight...
Cuz I can't stop thinking about that dick...
Shit...so...obsessed...with daddy dearest...
My favorite cuz he's beyond fearless...
I feel safe when he's the nearest...

Last Night....
I stroked his ego AND let him hear it...
And he licked my body until I couldn't feel him...

Sound asleep....in his arms...I laid there and pretended...
He was my personal charm prince...& He was ALL mine....forever...

You see...in my mind...picture perfect storybook ending...
And every time I closed my eyes...
My imagination returned me back to the beginning,

I seen...The first glance...the first touch....the first fucking...
Sense of stability....a solid foundation....
I enjoyed trusting your energy...and you were well worth my patience...

As I laid there sleep, you noticed my body still shaking and...
You held me tighter...and stared in my face...
You made sure I was sound, and you tried to stay awake...

Last night...u sure took me to a better place...
AND I wasn't trying to win but it was an Amazing Race.

# Lose Control

He can't control himself around me…
And actually admitted this with his own actions…proudly…
Chest poked out…cleared his throat…he moaned loudly…
I came fast, see, it's cuz…it was this one thing he did…
The way he pulled my hair…aroused she…
I don't usually swear so casually…Fuck…

But it's weird…you know…how he…Gets worked up…in an instant…
Like my hands somehow have powers prolific…
And he doesn't have to say…
What his body language is spitting…

Something about my bae is different… Soft shakes when we touch…
And we caress with intention…
The line is thin between lust… And Divine intervention…
The way he begs me for lunch, I love sexual ambition…
Feed him 3 times a day…

I fill him up...wet his lips and...
He pulls me tighter... Rearranges my position...
Strokes his tongue faster, harder and Holds me down from shifting...
And I really want to run....

I get so embarrassed by my liquids...
Soak up all of everything...

Once he figures what the trick is...
I leave the surface glistening...In an instant....
He's listening to moans barely falling off my lips and...
Of course...he's somehow empowered by this...

Before the long strokes begin...
He stands back and admires his workmanship...
Serenades his love with his best verses next...
Like Fleeeeeex....time to have seeeex......
and then there's the real test...
I gotta throw it back...let him know Reign's the best...

# Tasty Treats

Tasty Treats and tantalizing visuals
sensual aromas, erotic principals.

No rules…safe words…sweet songs…
Like that from those of a caged bird.

Released from the bondages of lives dramas…
Freeing our minds, our spirits fly through the night…
Dancing in the stars of righteousness.

Surrounded by the arts that our Father has created…
Our loves elevated.

Existing on higher planes than most,
I become so engulfed in you.

You become an image tatted on my memory.
So absolutely friendly, with divine intensity.

Warm kisses to all parts of your neck…
Relaxed…Refreshed…Deep Breaths…
Inhale the blessings and exhale the stress
And continue to get lost with me.

I'm feeling you more than my arms can reach…
Even with 2 pair of shades it ain't hard to see…
Love was made for us and you were sent to me.
I try to only return to reality…occasionally.

I enjoy the ride to wherever you're taking me.
And, sometimes my legs get to shaking. See?
I know a lot can happen from point a to b.

The human touch is a dangerous thing.
Goosebumps and spines shivering.
Natural reactions from the way your tongues delivering.

Whispering sweet things in my earlobes.
Stroking my chakras while you're rubbing my temples.
Reciting knowledge from our past kin folks.
Exchanging wisdom while we lay in between sheet folds
and bed spreads.

Early morning conversations including a nude breakfast, like
Feeding each other waffles and blindfold fruit tests.

# Wait

I'm making you wait because I'm worth it.
My actions support this.

Might play around sometimes,
Just temporarily alluring.
Picking a King wise
With genuine eyes,
Fit for a sexual Queen,
Also one,
With whom I can vibe.

And I can't front,
I have a special soft spot
For an intellectual thug..

I know that the one that's for me
Is full of compassion AND knows how to love.
He…surrenders to passion
And…not Just a great fuck.

I can take myself from zero to sixty
In the quickest of instants.
Pulling toys out of the bag,
And for fun, I slow lick them.
Just letting you know love,
So you don't get it twisted.

I'm making you wait, until the animal in me, kicks in.
And I'm holding onto my heart,
and all of my tongue tricks.

# Simplicity

Have you ever seen simplicity in its entirety?
You and me…the complicated irony.

Sometimes it seems,
Shit's just perfect.
Like, early Adam and Eve
Before the whole tree scheme.
Our secret gardens supreme.

For you, I would do anything.
Allow you to plow my fields
While we proudly raise these seeds,
And it's essential that you feel
Ever letter that I speak,
Combined with the sounds that make them unique.

I don't just use nouns
To explain things,
But, I'll tell you right now
That you are amazing.

I can't get enough.
Your mere touch,
Can just save me
From when the world is too much.

Thats' why I remind you daily
That you're my baby.

Tell you off rip..
If I notice one of ya peoples is shady.

Carry myself, in a way
That makes you proud that I'm your lady.

Busting rounds of knowledge
At these ignorant-ass babies.

To tell you the truth,
I've been mighty gansta lately.

With the heels on though,
And my fingernails red painted.
And I must be your type
Cuz your tongue seemed elated,

When I finally lost control,
And soaked your face while you ate it.
I felt that French kiss get intense
I just ain't say shit…
You know, its kind of hard at that time,
For any kind of conversation.

# Throat Hugging

I need you to understand…it ain't the truth until its ugly.
Let my throat do the hugging.

My mouth stays stupid wet now, ain't that lovely?
Shhhhh…shut up and just fuck me.

If it ain't room in your heart,
At least role play that you love me.

I can't get enough, I guess with you…
It's pure gluttony.

And I should mind but I don't cuz….
You do all the right things to keep me from running.

# Head Games

With the head games we play,
We should be ashamed.

For grown ups its supposed to be lame,
To engage in such a fashion.

So right now I'm asking.
Only play with my body,
Is that what you call Mackin?
I mean, could some smooth words
And a soft beat really make it happen?

Could I entice you with some pornetry,
Then perhaps an ass clap?
Spin my flesh not my mental,
The concept really is quite simple.

Let down your guard,
Allow me a little bit of space to jump into.
Ups and downs are okay but, let's keep it in the bedroom.

I smooth cuddle when I lay, but still bet you get head soon.
Be bold and be brave
Nothing is off limits, my mouth is without shame.
Allow my tongue to circle some of your areas…that keep shade.

Don't be scuuuurrrred…Aint no one
Trying to steal your manhood away.
So…give it up and quit playing.
I want to see which way your pipe lay.

# Can't Swim

I want to lick you in your favorite spot.
Find out the places that are ticklish or not.

Let your words be the guide
For my next couple of actions.

Whisper parts of your body
You want these kisses to happen,
And my lips can touch parts of MY flesh too…
Both nipples in my mouth at the same time for you.

Slow stroking my clit,
My wetness exudes.
So I'll poke my chest out
and I'll squeeze it too.

Let me grind on your nose just to prove.
I got strength in these legs,
and stamina to boot.
And then when the burn takes control
and I lose,
I'll have to slide on ya lips….
or I win?

I dunno….something happens to..
Reality when you start translating passion,
And I'll damn near drown you….
If you….can't swim.

# I Still Taste You

Mmmmm…I can still taste you.
My mind's tried to erase too,
But I can't.

I can still taste…
Our last episode on the stairway.
I'm not sure how YOU seem to be the one
That lingers on my upper lip &
Somehow manages to stay there…

I lose it…
I flip.
Anxious.

I love you in my mouth…
And I insist you abuse it &
If it's the skin flute,
I woke up and played music.
And then put you back to sleep,

Now…Thats the cool shit…
What more could YOU wish?

In the morning I served breakfast with a note.
Then washed you from your head to your toes.
Yes! I lathered you up with liquid peppermint soap.
Tingled your body…

You felt exposed.
Heart on your sleeve,
Your dick in between…
Your emotions and reality.

But I lick my lips and I taste you.
Matter of fact…see…
This situation is painful,
But, I've studied all angles…
And the sum of the equation…
Is that for you I am grateful…
For you I am able…
To do the impossible.

You Pinocchio my strings and I don't want to stop you.
My legs shake when you cream.
Looks crazy from the top view.
I used to silently scream…
Bite the pillow…
Now I rock…YOU!
Thats the cold truth.
AND something to get used to.

I've been consistent with the treatment,
Cuz I love to dome…
I mean this.
I made my mouth you home,
You let me bathe your penis.

Let me sow my royal oats, with my tongue…
Deliver slow strokes,
Creating small ejaculation.

Love to see you master patience.
I lick my lips, and I still taste it.
And the smile instantly raises…
The situations automatically changes…
The mood re-arranges.
But, the one thing that remains is….
I can only remember a taste.

If I could rewind time to the place…
Where you were pressed against my face…
The moments when I moaned your name.
The last time,
Back to back brain…
Insane….

But well..you know….
That's REIGN.

Next time…
Record me while I do my Thang..
My two paw grip, curls ya toes, Man!
I ghost rides the whip…
And do it with no hands…

Damn…
I'm still tasting my number one fan…
That man…truly….truly…does withstand…

So, peace my brotha…til we greet again…

# Let You Go

I know I need to let you go…
I know I do…
but I feel so strongly that I need to make love to you
one more good time…

Just one more time before I can see me just putting you back down…
Before I can completely detach myself from you…

I have never been so satisfied by pleasing someone else…
I have never gone so over the top to keep ANYONE happy…

It's not even possible for me to continue the pace
that I had predetermined as OUR speed…
Where I already know what it is you desire…
and before you know it's in front of your fave…

No one has made my heart smile
Without doing anything…ANYTHING…

I enjoyed…cooking and cleaning for you…day after day…
I enjoyed…tasting on you…day after day…
Even knowing that I had nothing coming in return…
and I never asked.

Nothing special…no gifts…no surprises…little conversations…
I knew you weren't going to cook…
I knew you were never going to come pick me up…
and shoot me out of a date…
You would probably never even suggest it…

I knew that I would spend my last
to make sure that you AND yours was ok…
And that me and mine probably weren't' even a thought to you…

I know that how I feel for you is so unhealthy…
because I cannot get you off of my brain…
But maybe…after one more occasion of laying in your arms
till the sun comes up…I could forget you…

Maybe if you wrap your arms around me
and rock me to sleep…one more time…
I could get over you…never think about you again…

At least I can say that you taught me something…
You taught me that I can LOVE…
But the icebox over my heart …
that ONLY allowed a broth to come over and cook for me…
Only allowing company to come over to CLEAN my house…

It's not that you dogged me…cuz you didn't …
I just knew that I didn't have anything more coming…
I AM a Queen…and I treated you like a KING…
But it's clear you don't desire that responsibility.
hmpf…

# Alignement

There's never a dull moment with you in my life….
I've been enjoying being single…
But if you asked me…
I wouldn't hesitate..
Turning into your wife…
Converting the QUEENDOM into a palace
KING-SIZED…
As strong as you are…
You can deal with my type….
Atomic energy when our spirits align.

# Big Fan

The way you tuck me in at night…
Allows the light of the morning to shine extra bright
I'm warning you…I am going to bite..when the chance is right.

Catch flights…and touchdown…
Let's face each other right now….right now.

Can't wait to land in your hometown…
And put these arms and legs around…your body…

Recently…for some reason…
My pure thoughts..have been spiked with naughty…
My eyes close…and your voice…charms see…
I want you more and more everyday…I am addicted…
The red flags don't seem to alarm me…

I can't seem to get enough…
Of your quick busts…
Back our conversations…Amazing…
In that…we go from relaxed to laughs…
Exchange moans and photographs…
Then back to a general ass…
Kiss through the phone…

I'm so glad…
We've made time for each other…
I'm gone…
Cuz what my mind says…
Is that my body should be right there with you…
At this exact moment…a case of a simple distance issue…

In truth…I ain't scared of shit…is you???

But every night…
Every night our back and forth…
Makes me wake up and want more…
They say every day a star is born…
I'm such a big fan of yours.

# Only Gets Better

Every time it only gets better…
My kitty is more wet…
Our back and forth is clever…

You talk your shit…and most the time…
I just sit back and let you…
But I'd trade away a lot of memories…
Just so I wouldn't forget you…

I love that you're so into me…
Your creativity's deceptive…
Cold…..Smoooooooth…

I guess it's….
The way you were raised…
Watched your father work two jobs…
To make sure that ya'll had food to scrape…
Every night up off ya plates…

And I'm gonna sit back and behave…
Let you be the man I need…
I'll let you wear the pants, believe…
Butt-naked while I dance, palm trees…

Catch a flight out to France…call me…
Madam Moiselle…
Beyonce isn't the only one alarming…

At night…I blow his horn and he…
Becomes a single one man army…
Attacking my body with passion…
I can hardly take it…

Way before…anything happens…
I'm shaking…my moans…
Vibrating off of every object…
In their way….

And each and every single time it…
Only gets better.

# Tension

I see it in your face, the tension.
Let me help you erase everything that needs missing.
Replace everything with my lips kiss, while,
Massaging ya back, with my French tips.

Every time we make love, I swim in visions.
So caught up in you, the bedroom seems endless.
I'm like the smallest part in this utopian village.
Where it's only you and I living,
Like the Garden of Eden
and it's only us eating..
69 ways…believe it.
and
It's a turn-on to smell me on your lips while you're breathing.
Inhaling myself gets me excited for some reason.
And tasting my juices on your chin is intriguing.

Maybe that's why…when you call begging…
It sounds more like you're actually feenin'…
For a hit of my honey or to taste of my seasons…

It's not until we cum together that we both feel complete.
When it's with you it's just better….I love the way that we freak…

So allow me to relax you please.
My tongue glides on everything.
My thighs cream imagining…
You fulfilling my dreams, somehow my kitty be ahead of me.
Already soaking, instantly.
Before you get to enter she.

People say, "Damn Reign, how many ways
can you really describe intimacy?"
However many ways it takes, see?

I put down my pen…and my iPad doesn't take ink.
So…shhhh…..and just kindly allow me to place
my tongue on your privacies.
It's that exact moment that my mind is the most free…

So many thoughts going on up there normally,
I be needing like 60 minutes to really
Address your microphone thoroughly.
I understand I gotta problem.
Cuz when it cums to ya dick,
Its a real sense of urgency.

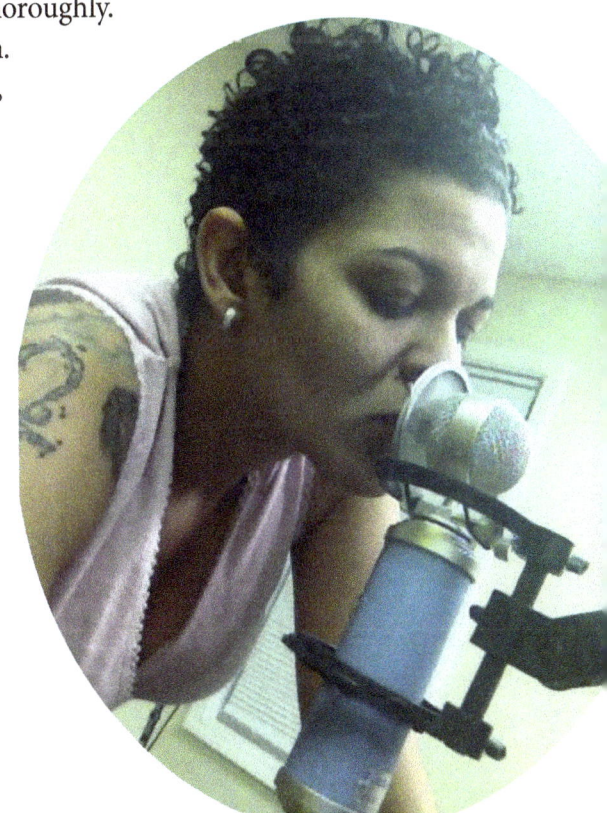

www.ingramcontent.com/pod-product-compliance
Lightning Source LLC
Chambersburg PA
CBHW061805070526
44586CB00023B/2715